PARIS

SHOPPING GUIDE 2024

A FRIENDLY GUIDE TO THE BEST SHOPPING IN THE CITY

PIERRE D. DUBOIS

PARIS SHOPPING GUIDE 2024
Discover the best shopping destinations and insider tips for a memorable experience.

ISBN-13: 9798853265998

INTRODUCTION

This Paris guide will help to discover the best shopping destinations and insider tips for a memorable experience.

The book includes a wide variety of stores ranging from high-end luxury boutiques to quirky independent shops, as well as markets and department stores.

The guide lists addresses, telephones, opening hours, information for tourists, curiosities, facts, how to get to each place and the attractions that are nearby.

Paris Shopping Guide 2024 is an excellent companion for anyone looking to discover the best shopping experiences that Paris has to offer.

AVENUE MONTAIGNE

This avenue is one of the most prestigious shopping destinations in Paris, lined with high-end fashion boutiques and designer brands.

Address: Avenue Montaigne, 75008 Paris, France

Amenities: Luxury shopping, cafes, restaurants

Stores and Brands: Dior, Chanel, Louis Vuitton, Gucci, Prada, and more

Advice: Come prepared to splurge, as prices for the luxury items here can be quite steep.

Tips: If you're on a budget, consider window shopping or checking out the less expensive shops and cafes nearby.

Review: Avenue Montaigne is a must-visit for fashion lovers and anyone looking to indulge in high-end shopping.

Getting there: The nearest metro stations are Alma-Marceau and Franklin D. Roosevelt.

BOULEVARD HAUSSMANN

Boulevard Haussmann is one of the busiest shopping areas in Paris, home to several department stores and high-street brands.

Address: Boulevard Haussmann, 75009 Paris, France

Amenities: Shopping, cafes, restaurants

Stores and Brands: Printemps, Galeries Lafayette, Zara, H&M, and more

Advice: Plan to spend a full day exploring the stores and sights along Boulevard Haussmann.

Tips: Check out the rooftop terrace of Galeries Lafayette for a stunning view of the city.

Review: Boulevard Haussmann is a great place to find everything from high-end luxury items to affordable fashion and accessories.

Getting there: The nearest metro stations are Chaussée d'Antin-La Fayette, Opéra, and Saint-Augustin.

BOULEVARD SAINT-GERMAIN

Boulevard Saint-Germain is a popular shopping area in Paris, known for its fashion boutiques, art galleries, and bookstores.

Address: Boulevard Saint-Germain, 75006 Paris, France

Amenities: Shopping, cafes, restaurants, cultural attractions

Stores and Brands: Yves Saint Laurent, Sonia Rykiel, Isabel Marant, and more

Advice: Take some time to explore the side streets and alleys off Boulevard Saint-Germain, as they often have hidden gems.

Tips: Check out the famous Cafe de Flore and Les Deux Magots, both popular hangouts for writers and artists.

Review: Boulevard Saint-Germain offers a mix of high-end fashion and independent boutiques, making it a great destination for anyone looking for unique and eclectic items.

Getting there: The nearest metro stations are Saint-Germain-des-Prés and Mabillon.

CHAMPS-ÉLYSÉES

Champs-Élysées is one of the most famous and iconic shopping streets in Paris, lined with luxury boutiques, cafes, and cinemas.

Address: Champs-Élysées, 75008 Paris, France

Amenities: Shopping, cafes, restaurants, cinemas

Stores and Brands: Louis Vuitton, Cartier, Sephora, H&M, and more

Advice: Be prepared for crowds and busy streets, as Champs-Élysées is a popular destination for tourists and locals alike.

Tips: Visit at night to see the famous avenue lit up with twinkling lights.

Review: Champs-Élysées is a must-visit for anyone looking to experience the glamour and luxury of Parisian shopping.

Getting there: The nearest metro stations are Franklin D. Roosevelt, Champs-Élysées-Clemenceau, and George V.

FAUBOURG SAINT-HONORÉ

Faubourg Saint-Honoré is a street in Paris known for its luxury fashion boutiques and designer stores.

Address: Faubourg Saint-Honoré, 75008 Paris, France

Amenities: Luxury shopping, cafes, restaurants

Stores and Brands: Hermès, Gucci, Lanvin, Christian Louboutin, and more

Advice: If you're on a budget, consider browsing the shops for inspiration and admiring the window displays.

Tips: Check out the nearby Place Vendôme for even more luxury shopping and the famous Ritz Paris hotel.

Review: Faubourg Saint-Honoré is a must-visit for anyone looking to indulge in high-end fashion and luxury shopping.

Getting there: The nearest metro stations are Concorde, Madeleine, and Saint-Philippe du Roule.

FORUM DES HALLES

Forum des Halles is a large shopping mall in the heart of Paris, with a wide range of stores and brands.

Address: Forum des Halles, 101 Porte Berger, 75001 Paris, France

Amenities: Shopping, cafes, restaurants, cinema, indoor garden

Stores and Brands: H&M, Zara, Sephora, Adidas, and more

Advice: Check out the recently renovated and expanded mall for a modern shopping experience.

Tips: Visit the rooftop terrace for a view of the surrounding area, and check out the nearby Saint-Eustache Church for a glimpse of Parisian history.

Review: Forum des Halles is a great destination for anyone looking for a variety of stores and brands in a modern and convenient location.

Getting there: The nearest metro station is Châtelet-Les Halles, which is also a major transportation hub in Paris.

GALERIES LAFAYETTE

Galeries Lafayette is a famous department store in Paris, known for its impressive glass dome and luxury fashion offerings.

Address: 40 Boulevard Haussmann, 75009 Paris, France

Amenities: Shopping, cafes, restaurants, panoramic terrace

Stores and Brands: Chanel, Dior, Louis Vuitton, Prada, and more

Advice: Don't miss the stunning views from the rooftop terrace, which offers panoramic views of the city.

Tips: Check out the free fashion shows and events that take place regularly in the store.

Review: Galeries Lafayette is a must-visit for anyone looking for a luxurious and impressive shopping experience in Paris.

Getting there: The nearest metro stations are Chaussée d'Antin-La Fayette and Opéra.

LE BON MARCHÉ

Le Bon Marché is a historic department store in Paris, known for its high-end fashion offerings and luxurious shopping experience.

Address: 24 Rue de Sèvres, 75007 Paris, France

Amenities: Shopping, cafes, restaurants, beauty and spa services

Stores and Brands: Saint Laurent, Céline, Fendi, Givenchy, and more

Advice: Take some time to explore the store's unique architecture and design, which includes stunning art installations and a central atrium.

Tips: Check out the nearby Rue du Cherche-Midi for even more high-end fashion boutiques.

Review: Le Bon Marché is a must-visit for anyone looking for a luxurious and unique shopping experience in Paris.

Getting there: The nearest metro stations are Sèvres-Babylone and Vaneau.

LE MARAIS

Le Marais is a trendy and fashionable neighborhood in Paris, known for its independent boutiques, vintage stores, and stylish cafes.

Address: Le Marais, 75003 Paris, France

Amenities: Shopping, cafes, restaurants, cultural attractions

Stores and Brands: Sandro, Maje, The Kooples, A.P.C., and more

Advice: Take your time to explore the small streets and alleys of Le Marais, as there are many hidden gems and unique stores to discover.

Tips: Check out the Marché aux Puces de Saint-Ouen, a nearby flea market that is a popular destination for vintage and antique shopping.

Review: Le Marais is a must-visit for anyone looking for a unique and stylish shopping experience in Paris.

Getting there: The nearest metro stations are Saint-Paul and Hôtel de Ville.

LE VILLAGE ROYAL

Le Village Royal is a small pedestrian street in the heart of Paris, known for its luxury fashion boutiques and charming atmosphere.

Address: Le Village Royal, 25 Rue Royale, 75008 Paris, France

Amenities: Luxury shopping, cafes, restaurants

Stores and Brands: Lanvin, Chloe, Prada, Giuseppe Zanotti, and more

Advice: Take some time to relax and enjoy the charming atmosphere of this hidden gem in the heart of Paris.

Tips: Check out the nearby Place de la Concorde for a stunning view of the Champs-Élysées and the Eiffel Tower.

Review: Le Village Royal is a must-visit for anyone looking for a unique and charming shopping experience in Paris.

Getting there: The nearest metro station is Concorde.

LE VILLAGE SAINT-PAUL

Le Village Saint-Paul is a picturesque pedestrian street in the Marais neighborhood of Paris, known for its antique shops, art galleries, and charming atmosphere.

Address: Le Village Saint-Paul, 75004 Paris, France

Amenities: Antique shopping, art galleries, cafes

Stores and Brands: Vintage and antique shops, art galleries, and more

Advice: Take your time to explore the small alleys and hidden corners of Le Village Saint-

Paul, as there are many unique finds to discover.

Tips: Visit on a Sunday when the street is closed to traffic, allowing for a more peaceful and relaxed shopping experience.

Review: Le Village Saint-Paul is a must-visit for anyone looking for a unique and charming shopping experience in Paris.

Getting there: The nearest metro station is Saint-Paul.

LES HALLES

Les Halles is a large shopping complex in the heart of Paris, with a wide range of stores, restaurants, and entertainment options.

Address: Les Halles, 101 Porte Berger, 75001 Paris, France

Amenities: Shopping, cafes, restaurants, cinema, swimming pool

Stores and Brands: Fnac, H&M, Zara, Sephora, and more

Advice: Check out the recently renovated and expanded mall for a modern and convenient shopping experience.

Tips: Visit the nearby Saint-Eustache Church for a glimpse of Parisian history and architecture.

Review: Les Halles is a great destination for anyone looking for a variety of stores and entertainment options in a modern and convenient location.

Getting there: The nearest metro station is Châtelet-Les Halles, which is also a major transportation hub in Paris.

PASSAGE DU GRAND CERF

Passage du Grand Cerf is a historic covered passage in Paris, known for its charming architecture and unique shops.

Address: Passage du Grand Cerf, 145 Rue Saint-Denis, 75002 Paris, France

Amenities: Shopping, cafes, restaurants

Stores and Brands: Unique and eclectic shops, including a toy store, a bookstore, a jewelry store, and more

Advice: Take some time to admire the stunning architecture of the passage, which includes a beautiful glass roof and intricate ironwork.

Tips: Visit on a weekday for a more peaceful and relaxed shopping experience.

Review: Passage du Grand Cerf is a must-visit for anyone looking for a unique and charming shopping experience in Paris.

Getting there: The nearest metro station is Étienne Marcel.

PLACE DE LA CONCORDE

Place de la Concorde is one of the most famous public squares in Paris, known for its impressive fountains, statues, and historic significance.

Address: Place de la Concorde, 75008 Paris, France

Amenities: Sightseeing, cafes, restaurants

Advice: Take some time to explore the square and its surroundings, which include the nearby Jardin des Tuileries and the Champs-Élysées.

Tips: Visit at night when the square is lit up and the fountains are illuminated.

Review: Place de la Concorde is a must-visit for anyone interested in Parisian history and architecture, and makes for a great stop on a sightseeing tour of the city.

Getting there: The nearest metro stations are Concorde and Madeleine.

PLACE DE LA MADELEINE

Place de la Madeleine is a beautiful public square in Paris, known for its impressive architecture and charming atmosphere.

Address: Place de la Madeleine, 75008 Paris, France

Amenities: Sightseeing, cafes, restaurants

Advice: Take some time to explore the square and its surroundings, which include the nearby Église de la Madeleine and the luxury shopping street of Rue du Faubourg Saint-Honoré.

Tips: Visit on a Sunday when the square is closed to traffic, allowing for a more peaceful and relaxed experience.

Review: Place de la Madeleine is a must-visit for anyone interested in Parisian architecture and history, and makes for a great stop on a sightseeing tour of the city.

Getting there: The nearest metro station is Madeleine.

PLACE DES VICTOIRES

Place des Victoires is a beautiful public square in Paris, known for its impressive statue of King Louis XIV and its luxurious surroundings.

Address: Place des Victoires, 75001 Paris, France

Amenities: Sightseeing, cafes, restaurants

Stores and Brands: Luxury fashion boutiques, including Cartier, Hermès, and Yves Saint Laurent

Advice: Take some time to explore the square and its surroundings, which include the nearby Palais Royal and the trendy shopping street of Rue Saint-Honoré.

Tips: Visit at night when the square is lit up and the statue of King Louis XIV is illuminated.

Review: Place des Victoires is a must-visit for anyone interested in Parisian architecture and luxury fashion, and makes for a great stop on a sightseeing and shopping tour of the city.

Getting there: The nearest metro station is Bourse.

PLACE DES VOSGES

Place des Vosges is a beautiful public square in Paris, known for its impressive architecture, historic significance, and charming atmosphere.

Address: Place des Vosges, 75004 Paris, France

Amenities: Sightseeing, cafes, restaurants

Advice: Take some time to explore the square and its surroundings, which include the nearby Musée Carnavalet and the trendy shopping street of Rue des Francs-Bourgeois.

Tips: Visit on a sunny day when the square is filled with locals and tourists enjoying a picnic or a game of petanque.

Review: Place des Vosges is a must-visit for anyone interested in Parisian history, architecture, and culture, and makes for a great stop on a sightseeing tour of the city.

Getting there: The nearest metro stations are Saint-Paul and Bastille.

PLACE VENDÔME

Place Vendôme is a beautiful public square in Paris, known for its impressive architecture, luxury fashion boutiques, and high-end jewelry stores.

Address: Place Vendôme, 75001 Paris, France

Amenities: Luxury shopping, cafes, restaurants

Stores and Brands: Luxury fashion boutiques, including Chanel, Louis Vuitton, and Dior, as well as high-end jewelry stores, including Cartier and Van Cleef & Arpels

Advice: Take some time to admire the stunning architecture of the square, which includes a beautiful column topped by a statue of Napoleon.

Tips: Visit at night when the square is lit up and the luxury boutiques and jewelry stores are illuminated.

Review: Place Vendôme is a must-visit for anyone interested in luxury fashion and high-end jewelry, and makes for a great stop on a shopping tour of the city.

Getting there: The nearest metro stations are Opéra and Tuileries.

PRINTEMPS

Printemps is a historic department store in Paris, known for its impressive architecture, luxury shopping, and panoramic views of the city.

Address: Printemps, 64 Boulevard Haussmann, 75009 Paris, France

Amenities: Shopping, cafes, restaurants, panoramic views

Stores and Brands: Luxury fashion brands, including Chanel, Dior, and Gucci, as well as high-end beauty and home goods

Advice: Take some time to explore the various floors of the store, which offer a range of products and experiences, from fashion and beauty to food and drink.

Tips: Visit the rooftop terrace for stunning panoramic views of Paris.

Review: Printemps is a must-visit for anyone interested in luxury shopping and impressive architecture, and offers a unique and memorable shopping experience in the heart of Paris.

Getting there: The nearest metro stations are Havre-Caumartin and Auber.

RUE DE BELLEVILLE

Rue de Belleville is a vibrant and multicultural street in Paris, known for its affordable shopping, diverse food options, and lively atmosphere.

Address: Rue de Belleville, 75020 Paris, France

Amenities: Shopping, cafes, restaurants

Stores and Brands: Affordable fashion and accessories, including many Asian and African shops and boutiques

Advice: Take some time to explore the street and its surroundings, which include the nearby Parc de Belleville and the trendy neighborhood of Ménilmontant.

Tips: Visit on a Sunday when the street is closed to traffic, allowing for a more peaceful and relaxed experience.

Review: Rue de Belleville is a must-visit for anyone interested in affordable fashion and multicultural experiences, and offers a unique and lively shopping experience in the heart of Paris.

Getting there: The nearest metro stations are Belleville and Pyrénées.

RUE DE BRETAGNE

Rue de Bretagne is a trendy and lively street in Paris, known for its diverse food markets, fashionable boutiques, and charming atmosphere.

Address: Rue de Bretagne, 75003 Paris, France

Amenities: Shopping, food markets, cafes, restaurants

Stores and Brands: Trendy fashion boutiques, including Ba&sh and Vanessa

Bruno, as well as unique home goods and decor shops

Advice: Take some time to explore the food markets, including the famous Marché des Enfants Rouges, which offers a range of international cuisine and fresh produce.

Tips: Visit on a Sunday when the street is closed to traffic, allowing for a more peaceful and relaxed experience.

Review: Rue de Bretagne is a must-visit for anyone interested in food markets, trendy boutiques, and a lively atmosphere, and offers a unique and memorable shopping experience in the heart of Paris.

Getting there: The nearest metro station is Filles du Calvaire.

RUE DE BUCI

Rue de Buci is a charming and historic street in Paris, known for its lively atmosphere, trendy boutiques, and quaint cafes.

Address: Rue de Buci, 75006 Paris, France

Amenities: Shopping, cafes, restaurants

Stores and Brands: Trendy fashion boutiques, including Sandro and Claudie Pierlot, as well as unique artisanal shops and bookstores

Advice: Take some time to explore the charming side streets and alleyways, which offer a range of shops and boutiques.

Tips: Visit at night when the street is lit up and the cafes and restaurants are filled with locals and tourists.

Review: Rue de Buci is a must-visit for anyone interested in charming and historic shopping streets, and offers a unique and lively atmosphere in the heart of Paris.

Getting there: The nearest metro station is Mabillon.

RUE DE CHARONNE

Rue de Charonne is a trendy and up-and-coming street in Paris, known for its unique and independent shops, bars, and restaurants.

Address: Rue de Charonne, 75011 Paris, France

Amenities: Shopping, bars, restaurants

Stores and Brands: Unique and independent shops and boutiques, including vintage clothing and artisanal goods

Advice: Take some time to explore the side streets and alleys, which offer a range of unique and interesting shops and bars.

Tips: Visit on a weekend when the street is bustling with locals and tourists, and check out some of the trendy bars and restaurants in the area.

Review: Rue de Charonne is a must-visit for anyone interested in unique and independent shops and a lively nightlife scene, and offers a refreshing change of pace from the more touristy shopping streets in Paris.

Getting there: The nearest metro stations are Charonne and Ledru-Rollin.

RUE DE GRENELLE

Rue de Grenelle is a chic and upscale street in Paris, known for its high-end boutiques, art galleries, and charming atmosphere.

Address: Rue de Grenelle, 75007 Paris, France

Amenities: Shopping, art galleries, cafes, restaurants

Stores and Brands: High-end fashion boutiques, including Chloé and Stella McCartney, as well as luxury home goods and decor shops

Advice: Take some time to explore the charming side streets and alleyways, which offer a range of boutiques and art galleries.

Tips: Visit the nearby Musée Rodin to see some of the artist's most famous sculptures and works of art.

Review: Rue de Grenelle is a must-visit for anyone interested in high-end fashion and luxury shopping, and offers a charming and refined shopping experience in the heart of Paris.

Getting there: The nearest metro station is Rue du Bac.

RUE DE L'UNIVERSITÉ

Rue de l'Université is a charming and historic street in Paris, known for its upscale boutiques, art galleries, and elegant architecture.

Address: Rue de l'Université, 75007 Paris, France

Amenities: Shopping, art galleries, cafes, restaurants

Stores and Brands: High-end fashion boutiques, including Saint Laurent and Lanvin, as well as luxury home goods and decor shops

Advice: Take some time to explore the nearby Musée d'Orsay and its collection of impressionist and post-impressionist art.

Tips: Visit on a weekday when the street is quieter and the boutiques and art galleries are less crowded.

Review: Rue de l'Université is a must-visit for anyone interested in high-end fashion and luxury shopping, and offers a charming and refined shopping experience in one of the most elegant neighborhoods in Paris.

Getting there: The nearest metro stations are Rue du Bac and Solférino.

RUE DE L'ÉCHIQUIER

Rue de l'Échiquier is a trendy and up-and-coming street in Paris, known for its independent shops, bars, and restaurants.

Address: Rue del'Échiquier, 75010 Paris, France

Amenities: Shopping, bars, restaurants

Stores and Brands: Independent shops and boutiques, including vintage clothing and artisanal goods

Advice: Take some time to explore the charming side streets and alleys, which offer a range of unique and interesting shops and bars.

Tips: Visit in the evening when the street is bustling with locals and tourists enjoying the nightlife scene.

Review: Rue de l'Échiquier is a must-visit for anyone interested in unique and independent shops and a lively nightlife scene, and offers a refreshing change of pace from the more touristy shopping streets in Paris.

Getting there: The nearest metro stations are Bonne Nouvelle and Strasbourg-Saint-Denis.

RUE DE L'ÉGLISE

Rue de l'Église is a charming and historic street in Paris, known for its quaint shops, cafes, and cobblestone streets.

Address: Rue de l'Église, 75015 Paris, France

Amenities: Shopping, cafes, restaurants

Stores and Brands: Quaint and charming boutiques and shops, including artisanal goods and unique gifts

Advice: Take some time to explore the nearby Parc Georges Brassens, which offers a tranquil escape from the city.

Tips: Visit on a Sunday when the street is closed to traffic and locals gather to enjoy the weekly market.

Review: Rue de l'Église is a must-visit for anyone interested in charming and historic shopping streets, and offers a unique and peaceful shopping experience in the heart of Paris.

Getting there: The nearest metro station is Convention.

RUE DE LA CHAUSSÉE D'ANTIN

Rue de la Chaussée d'Antin is a bustling and lively street in Paris, known for its department stores, fashion boutiques, and trendy cafes.

Address: Rue de la Chaussée d'Antin, 75009 Paris, France

Amenities: Shopping, cafes, restaurants

Stores and Brands: Department stores, including Galeries Lafayette and Printemps, as well as trendy fashion boutiques and luxury shops

Advice: Take some time to explore the nearby Palais Garnier, the stunning opera house that is one of Paris's most iconic landmarks.

Tips: Visit in the winter when the street is decorated with festive lights and displays.

Review: Rue de la Chaussée d'Antin is a must-visit for anyone interested in department stores and high-end fashion, and offers a lively and bustling shopping experience in one of Paris's most vibrant neighborhoods.

Getting there: The nearest metro stations are Chaussée d'Antin La Fayette and Opéra.

RUE DE LA CONVENTION

Rue de la Convention is a charming and lively street in Paris, known for its local shops, cafes, and friendly atmosphere.

Address: Rue de la Convention, 75015 Paris, France

Amenities: Shopping, cafes, restaurants

Stores and Brands: Local shops and boutiques, including artisanal goods and unique gifts

Advice: Take some time to explore the nearby Parc André Citroën, which offers a range of green spaces and attractions, including hot air balloon rides.

Tips: Visit on a Saturday when the street is bustling with locals enjoying the weekly market.

Review: Rue de la Convention is a must-visit for anyone interested in charming and local shopping streets, and offers a unique and friendly shopping experience in the heart of Paris.

Getting there: The nearest metro station is Convention.

RUE DE LA GRANGE BATELIÈRE

Rue de la Grange Batelière is a historic and charming street in Paris, known for its unique and independent shops and boutiques.

Address: Rue de la Grange Batelière, 75009 Paris, France

Amenities: Shopping, cafes, restaurants

Stores and Brands: Independent shops and boutiques, including vintage clothing and artisanal goods

Advice: Take some time to explore the nearby Musée Gustave Moreau, which offers a fascinating collection of art and artifacts in the artist's former home and studio.

Tips: Visit on a weekday when the street is quieter and the shops and boutiques are less crowded.

Review: Rue de la Grange Batelière is a must-visit for anyone interested in unique and independent shops, and offers a charming and historic shopping experience in the heart of Paris.

Getting there: The nearest metro station is Grands Boulevards.

RUE DE LA HARPE

Rue de la Harpe is a bustling and lively street in Paris, known for its shops, bars, and nightlife scene.

Address: Rue de la Harpe, 75005 Paris, France

Amenities: Shopping, bars, restaurants

Stores and Brands: Independent shops and boutiques, including vintage clothing and artisanal goods

Advice: Take some time to explore the nearby Luxembourg Gardens, which offer a tranquil escape from the city.

Tips: Visit in the evening when the street is bustling with locals and tourists enjoying the nightlife scene.

Review: Rue de la Harpe is a must-visit for anyone interested in unique and independent shops and a lively nightlife scene, and offers a refreshing change of pace from the more touristy shopping streets in Paris.

Getting there: The nearest metro stations are Cluny-La Sorbonne and Saint-Michel Notre-Dame.

RUE DE LA PAIX

Rue de la Paix is one of Paris's most prestigious shopping streets, known for its luxury boutiques and high-end fashion.

Address: Rue de la Paix, 75002 Paris, France

Amenities: Shopping, cafes, restaurants

Stores and Brands: Luxury fashion boutiques, including Cartier, Chanel, and Louis Vuitton

Advice: Take some time to explore the nearby Place Vendôme, a stunning square known for its historic architecture and luxury boutiques.

Tips: Visit in the winter when the street is decorated with festive lights and displays.

Review: Rue de la Paix is a must-visit for anyone interested in luxury fashion and high-end shopping, and offers a glamorous and sophisticated shopping experience in the heart of Paris.

Getting there: The nearest metro stations are Opéra and Madeleine.

RUE DE LA POMPE

Rue de la Pompe is a charming and historic street in Paris, known for its unique and independent shops and boutiques.

Address: Rue de la Pompe, 75116 Paris, France

Amenities: Shopping, cafes, restaurants

Stores and Brands: Independent shops and boutiques, including vintage clothing and artisanal goods

Advice: Take some time to explore the nearby Bois de Boulogne, a sprawling park with a range of outdoor activities and attractions.

Tips: Visit on a weekday when the street is quieter and the shops and boutiques are less crowded.

Review: Rue de la Pompe is a must-visit for anyone interested in unique and independent shops, and offers a charming and historic shopping experience in the heart of Paris's 16th arrondissement.

Getting there: The nearest metro station is Rue de la Pompe.

RUE DE LA RO

Rue de la Ro is a charming and historic street in Paris, known for its local shops and independent boutiques.

Address: Rue de la Ro, 75001 Paris, France

Amenities: Shopping, cafes, restaurants

Stores and Brands: Independent shops and boutiques, including artisanal goods and unique gifts

Advice: Take some time to explore the nearby Louvre Museum, one of the world's most famous museums and home to an incredible collection of art and artifacts.

Tips: Visit on a Sunday when the street is closed to traffic and filled with a festive atmosphere.

Review: Rue de la Ro is a must-visit for anyone interested in charming and local shopping streets, and offers a unique and friendly shopping experience in the heart of Paris.

Getting there: The nearest metro station is Palais Royal-Musée du Louvre.

RUE DE LA ROQUETTE

Rue de la Roquette is a lively and trendy street in Paris, known for its unique and independent shops, cafes, and nightlife.

Address: Rue de la Roquette, 75011 Paris, France

Amenities: Shopping, cafes, restaurants, nightlife

Stores and Brands: Independent shops and boutiques, including vintage clothing and artisanal goods

Advice: Take some time to explore the nearby Père Lachaise Cemetery, a historic cemetery and the final resting place of many famous artists and thinkers.

Tips: Visit in the evening when the street comes alive with trendy bars and restaurants.

Review: Rue de la Roquette is a must-visit for anyone interested in unique and independent shops and trendy nightlife, and offers a refreshing change of pace from the more touristy shopping streets in Paris.

Getting there: The nearest metro stations are Bastille and Voltaire.

RUE DE LAPPE

Rue de Lappe is a vibrant and lively street in Paris, known for its bars, clubs, and nightlife scene.

Address: Rue de Lappe, 75011 Paris, France

Amenities: Nightlife, bars, restaurants

Stores and Brands: Independent shops and boutiques, including vintage clothing and artisanal goods

Advice: Take some time to explore the nearby Marais district, a historic neighborhood with a range of shops, restaurants, and cultural attractions.

Tips: Visit in the evening when the street is bustling with locals and tourists enjoying the nightlife scene.

Review: Rue de Lappe is a must-visit for anyone interested in trendy bars and a lively nightlife scene, and offers a fun and energetic atmosphere in the heart of Paris.

Getting there: The nearest metro stations are Bastille and Ledru-Rollin.

RUE DE MONTMARTRE

Rue de Montmartre is a charming and historic street in Paris, known for its local shops and boutiques.

Address: Rue de Montmartre, 75002 Paris, France

Amenities: Shopping, cafes, restaurants

Stores and Brands: Independent shops and boutiques, including artisanal goods and unique gifts

Advice: Take some time to explore the nearby Montmartre district, a historic neighborhood with a range of shops, restaurants, and cultural attractions.

Tips: Visit on a weekday when the street is quieter and the shops and boutiques are less crowded.

Review: Rue de Montmartre is a must-visit for anyone interested in charming and local shopping streets, and offers a unique and friendly shopping experience in the heart of Paris.

Getting there: The nearest metro stations are Grands Boulevards and Sentier.

RUE DE PASSY

Rue de Passy is a stylish and elegant street in Paris, known for its high-end boutiques and luxury shopping.

Address: Rue de Passy, 75016 Paris, France

Amenities: Shopping, cafes, restaurants

Stores and Brands: Luxury fashion boutiques, including Hermès and Cartier

Advice: Take some time to explore the nearby Bois de Boulogne, a sprawling park with a range of outdoor activities and attractions.

Tips: Visit in the summer when the street is decorated with beautiful flower arrangements.

Review: Rue de Passy is a must-visit for anyone interested in luxury fashion and high-end shopping, and offers a glamorous and sophisticated shopping experience in the heart of Paris's 16th arrondissement.

Getting there: The nearest metro station is Passy.

RUE DE RIVOLI

Rue de Rivoli is one of Paris's most famous shopping streets, known for its wide range of shops and boutiques.

Address: Rue de Rivoli, 75001 Paris, France

Amenities: Shopping, cafes, restaurants

Stores and Brands: High street shops, including H&M and Zara, and luxury boutiques, including Chanel and Dior

Advice: Take some time to explore the nearby Tuileries Garden, a beautiful park with a range of outdoor activities and attractions.

Tips: Visit in the evening when the street is lit up and has a magical atmosphere.

Review: Rue de Rivoli is a must-visit for anyone interested in shopping in Paris, and offers a wide range of shops and boutiques to suit every taste and budget.

Getting there: The nearest metro stations are Châtelet and Tuileries.

RUE DE SEINE

Rue de Seine is a charming and historic street in Paris, known for its local shops and boutiques.

Address: Rue de Seine, 75006 Paris, France

Amenities: Shopping, cafes, restaurants

Stores and Brands: Independent shops and boutiques, including artisanal goods and unique gifts

Advice: Take some time to explore the nearby Saint-Germain-des-Prés neighborhood, a historic district with a range of shops, restaurants, and cultural attractions.

Tips: Visit on a Sunday when the street is closed to traffic and filled with a festive atmosphere.

Review: Rue de Seine is a must-visit for anyone interested in charming and local shopping streets, and offers a unique and friendly shopping experience in the heart of Paris.

Getting there: The nearest metro stations are Mabillon and Odéon.

RUE DE SOLFÉRINO

Rue de Solférino is a chic and upscale street in Paris, known for its luxury boutiques and elegant architecture.

Address: Rue de Solférino, 75007 Paris, France

Amenities: Shopping, cafes, restaurants

Stores and Brands: Luxury fashion boutiques, including Yves Saint Laurent and Isabel Marant

Advice: Take some time to explore the nearby Musée d'Orsay, a world-renowned museum featuring a collection of Impressionist and Post-Impressionist masterpieces.

Tips: Visit in the spring when the street is adorned with beautiful blossoms.

Review: Rue de Solférino is a must-visit for anyone interested in luxury fashion and high-end shopping, and offers a glamorous and sophisticated shopping experience in the heart of Paris's 7th arrondissement.

Getting there: The nearest metro station is Solférino.

RUE DE SÈVRES

Rue de Sèvres is a stylish and elegant street in Paris, known for its high-end boutiques and luxury shopping.

Address: Rue de Sèvres, 75006 Paris, France

Amenities: Shopping, cafes, restaurants

Stores and Brands: Luxury fashion boutiques, including Hermès and Saint Laurent

Advice: Take some time to explore the nearby Luxembourg Gardens, a beautiful park with a range of outdoor activities and attractions.

Tips: Visit in the winter when the street is decorated with beautiful holiday lights.

Review: Rue de Sèvres is a must-visit for anyone interested in luxury fashion and high-end shopping, and offers a glamorous and sophisticated shopping experience in the heart of Paris's 6th arrondissement.

Getting there: The nearest metro stations are Sèvres-Babylone and Saint-Sulpice.

RUE DE TOLBIAC

Rue de Tolbiac is a bustling and vibrant street in Paris, known for its local shops and international cuisine.

Address: Rue de Tolbiac, 75013 Paris, France

Amenities: Shopping, cafes, restaurants

Stores and Brands: Independent shops and boutiques, including specialty food stores and artisanal crafts

Advice: Take some time to explore the nearby Chinatown district, a lively neighborhood with a range of shops, restaurants, and cultural attractions.

Tips: Visit on a Saturday when the street is filled with a bustling market.

Review: Rue de Tolbiac is a must-visit for anyone interested in local and international shopping and cuisine, and offers a unique and diverse shopping experience in the heart of Paris's 13th arrondissement.

Getting there: The nearest metro station is Tolbiac.

RUE DE TURENNE

Rue de Turenne is a trendy and fashionable street in Paris, known for its local designers and unique boutiques.

Address: Rue de Turenne, 75003 Paris, France

Amenities: Shopping, cafes, restaurants

Stores and Brands: Local designers and independent boutiques, including vintage clothing and handmade goods

Advice: Take some time to explore the nearby Marais district, a historic neighborhood with a range of shops, museums, and cultural attractions.

Tips: Visit on a Thursday when the street is filled with a lively market.

Review: Rue de Turenne is a must-visit for anyone interested in local and unique shopping experiences, and offers a range of creative and fashionable boutiques in the heart of Paris's 3rd arrondissement.

Getting there: The nearest metro station is Saint-Paul.

RUE DES ABBESSES

Rue des Abbesses is a charming and picturesque street in Paris, known for its local shops and cafes.

Address: Rue des Abbesses, 75018 Paris, France

Amenities: Shopping, cafes, restaurants

Stores and Brands: Local shops and boutiques, including artisanal food and handmade goods

Advice: Take some time to explore the nearby Montmartre district, a historic neighborhood with a range of shops, museums, and cultural attractions.

Tips: Visit in the spring when the street is adorned with beautiful blossoms.

Review: Rue des Abbesses is a must-visit for anyone interested in charming and local shopping streets, and offers a unique and friendly shopping experience in the heart of Paris's 18th arrondissement.

Getting there: The nearest metro station is Abbesses.

RUE DES ARCHIVES

Rue des Archives is a historic and stylish street in Paris, known for its local designers and vintage boutiques.

Address: Rue des Archives, 75004 Paris, France

Amenities: Shopping, cafes, restaurants

Stores and Brands: Local designers and vintage boutiques, including antique stores and unique gifts

Advice: Take some time to explore the nearby Le Marais district, a historic neighborhood with a range of shops, museums, and cultural attractions.

Tips: Visit on a Sunday when the street is closed to traffic and filled with a lively market.

Review: Rue des Archives is a must-visit for anyone interested in vintage and unique shopping experiences, and offers a range of creative and fashionable boutiques in the heart of Paris's 4th arrondissement.

Getting there: The nearest metro stations are Hôtel de Ville and Saint-Paul.

RUE DES BATIGNOLLES

Rue des Batignolles is a charming and peaceful street in Paris, known for its local shops and bakeries.

Address: Rue des Batignolles, 75017 Paris, France

Amenities: Shopping, cafes, restaurants

Stores and Brands: Local shops and boutiques, including artisanal food and handmade goods

Advice: Take some time to explore the nearby Batignolles district, a peaceful and friendly neighborhood with a range of shops, parks, and cultural attractions.

Tips: Visit in the fall when the street is lined with beautiful autumn leaves.

Review: Rue des Batignolles is a must-visit for anyone interested in charming and local shopping streets, and offers a unique and friendly shopping experience in the heart of Paris's 17th arrondissement.

Getting there: The nearest metro station is Rome.

RUE DES FRANCS-BOURGEOIS

Rue des Francs-Bourgeois is a trendy and fashionable street in Paris, known for its local designers and high-end boutiques.

Address: Rue des Francs-Bourgeois, 75003 Paris, France

Amenities: Shopping, cafes, restaurants

Stores and Brands: Local designers and high-end boutiques, including Chanel and Sandro

Advice: Take some time to explore the nearby Marais district, a historic neighborhood with a range of shops, museums, and cultural attractions.

Tips: Visit on a Sunday when the street is closed to traffic and filled with a lively market.

Review: Rue des Francs-Bourgeois is a must-visit for anyone interested in fashion and high-end shopping, and offers a range of creative and fashionable boutiques in the heart of Paris's 3rd arrondissement.

Getting there: The nearest metro stations are Saint-Paul and Chemin Vert.

RUE DES MARTYRS

Rue des Martyrs is a quaint and charming street in Paris, known for its local shops and artisanal food.

Address: Rue des Martyrs, 75009 Paris, France

Amenities: Shopping, cafes, restaurants

Stores and Brands: Local shops and boutiques, including artisanal food, bakeries, and independent fashion boutiques

Advice: Take some time to explore the nearby Montmartre district, a historic neighborhood with a range of shops, museums, and cultural attractions.

Tips: Visit in the morning to sample some of the local bakeries and food shops.

Review: Rue des Martyrs is a must-visit for anyone interested in charming and local shopping streets, and offers a unique and friendly shopping experience in the heart of Paris's 9th arrondissement.

Getting there: The nearest metro station is Pigalle.

RUE DES PETITS CARREAUX

Rue des Petits Carreaux is a bustling and lively street in Paris, known for its local shops and wholesale markets.

Address: Rue des Petits Carreaux, 75001 Paris, France

Amenities: Shopping, cafes, restaurants

Stores and Brands: Local shops and boutiques, including clothing, accessories, and artisanal food

Advice: Take some time to explore the nearby Les Halles district, a historic neighborhood with a range of shops, museums, and cultural attractions.

Tips: Visit in the afternoon when the street is filled with a lively market and street performers.

Review: Rue des Petits Carreaux is a must-visit for anyone interested in local and unique shopping experiences, and offers a range of creative and fashionable boutiques in the heart of Paris's 1st arrondissement.

Getting there: The nearest metro station is Sentier.

RUE DES PETITS CHAMPS

Rue des Petits Champs is a lively and bustling street in Paris, known for its mix of local shops, Asian cuisine, and historical landmarks.

Address: Rue des Petits Champs, 75001 Paris, France

Amenities: Shopping, cafes, restaurants, historical landmarks

Stores and Brands: Local shops and boutiques, including Asian markets and boutiques

Advice: Take some time to explore the nearby Palais-Royal gardens and museum, a beautiful and historic landmark in the heart of Paris.

Tips: Visit in the evening to sample some of the local Asian cuisine.

Review: Rue des Petits Champs offers a unique and vibrant shopping experience in the heart of Paris's 1st arrondissement, with a mix of local shops, Asian markets, and historical landmarks.

Getting there: The nearest metro station is Pyramides.

RUE DES PYRÉNÉES

Rue des Pyrénées is a charming and local street in Paris, known for its small shops, bakeries, and cafes.

Address: Rue des Pyrénées, 75020 Paris, France

Amenities: Shopping, cafes, restaurants

Stores and Brands: Local shops and boutiques, including bakeries and independent fashion boutiques

Advice: Take some time to explore the nearby Belleville district, a multicultural and friendly neighborhood with a range of shops, parks, and cultural attractions.

Tips: Visit in the morning to sample some of the local bakeries and cafes.

Review: Rue des Pyrénées is a must-visit for anyone interested in charming and local shopping streets, and offers a unique and friendly shopping experience in the heart of Paris's 20th arrondissement.

Getting there: The nearest metro station is Pyrénées.

RUE DES ROSIERS

Rue des Rosiers is a historic and lively street in Paris, known for its Jewish heritage, local shops, and street food.

Address: Rue des Rosiers, 75004 Paris, France

Amenities: Shopping, cafes, restaurants, historical landmarks

Stores and Brands: Local shops and boutiques, including traditional Jewish bakeries and fashion boutiques

Advice: Take some time to explore the nearby Marais district, a historic neighborhood with a range of shops, museums, and cultural attractions.

Tips: Visit on a Sunday when the street is closed to traffic and filled with a lively market.

Review: Rue des Rosiers is a must-visit for anyone interested in exploring Paris's Jewish heritage and local shopping scene. The street offers a unique and lively atmosphere with a range of traditional Jewish bakeries, fashion boutiques, and street food stands.

Getting there: The nearest metro station is Saint-Paul.

RUE DU BAC

Rue du Bac is a chic and upscale street in Paris, known for its high-end fashion boutiques, art galleries, and gourmet food shops.

Address: Rue du Bac, 75007 Paris, France

Amenities: Shopping, cafes, restaurants, art galleries

Stores and Brands: High-end fashion boutiques and luxury brands, including Hermes, Prada, and Chanel

Advice: Take some time to explore the nearby Musée d'Orsay, a world-renowned museum with a stunning collection of impressionist and post-impressionist art.

Tips: Visit in the afternoon to sample some of the local gourmet food shops.

Review: Rue du Bac offers a unique and luxurious shopping experience in the heart of Paris's 7th arrondissement, with a range of high-end fashion boutiques, art galleries, and gourmet food shops.

Getting there: The nearest metro station is Rue du Bac.

RUE DU CHERCHE-MIDI

Rue du Cherche-Midi is a charming and local street in Paris, known for its mix of independent fashion boutiques, vintage shops, and artisanal food.

Address: Rue du Cherche-Midi, 75006 Paris, France

Amenities: Shopping, cafes, restaurants

Stores and Brands: Independent fashion boutiques, vintage shops, and artisanal food shops

Advice: Take some time to explore the nearby Saint-Germain-des-Prés district, a historic and cultural neighborhood with a range of shops, museums, and art galleries.

Tips: Visit in the morning to sample some of the local bakeries and cafes.

Review: Rue du Cherche-Midi is a must-visit for anyone interested in unique and local shopping experiences, and offers a mix of independent fashion boutiques, vintage shops, and artisanal food in the heart of Paris's 6th arrondissement.

Getting there: The nearest metro station is Saint-Sulpice.

RUE DU COMMERCE

Rue du Commerce is a local and bustling shopping street in Paris, known for its mix of local shops, restaurants, and cafes.

Address: Rue du Commerce, 75015 Paris, France

Amenities: Shopping, cafes, restaurants

Stores and Brands: Local shops selling clothing, accessories, and home goods, as well as larger retail stores like Zara and H&M

Advice: Don't miss out on exploring the nearby Parc André Citroën, a modern and green space in the heart of the 15th arrondissement with stunning views of the Eiffel Tower.

Tips: Visit on Sundays when the street is closed to traffic and becomes a pedestrian-only zone.

Review: Rue du Commerce offers a vibrant and local shopping experience in the heart of Paris's 15th arrondissement, with a range of local shops and larger retail stores like Zara and H&M. The street has a lively atmosphere, especially on Sundays when it becomes a pedestrian-only zone.

Getting there: The nearest metro station is Commerce.

RUE DU FAUBOURG-DU-TEMPLE

Rue du Faubourg-du-Temple is a local and diverse shopping street in Paris, known for its mix of independent shops, street art, and ethnic food.

Address: Rue du Faubourg-du-Temple, 75011 Paris, France

Amenities: Shopping, cafes, restaurants, street art

Stores and Brands: Independent shops selling clothing, accessories, and home goods, as well as ethnic food shops and street vendors

Advice: Explore the nearby Belleville neighborhood, known for its vibrant street art scene and diverse cultural offerings.

Tips: Visit in the afternoon to experience the street's lively atmosphere and street food vendors.

Review: Rue du Faubourg-du-Temple offers a unique and diverse shopping experience in the heart of Paris's 11th arrondissement, with a mix of independent shops, ethnic food, and street art. The street has a lively and vibrant atmosphere, especially in the afternoon when street food vendors set up their stalls.

Getting there: The nearest metro station is Goncourt.

RUE DU FAUBOURG-POISSONNIÈRE

Rue du Faubourg-Poissonnière is a local and authentic shopping street in Paris, known for its mix of local shops, restaurants, and bars.

Address: Rue du Faubourg-Poissonnière, 75010 Paris, France

Amenities: Shopping, cafes, restaurants, bars

Stores and Brands: Local shops selling clothing, accessories, and home goods, as well as specialty food shops and bakeries

Advice: Take some time to explore the nearby Grands Boulevards, a historic and lively neighborhood with a range of theaters, cafes, and shops.

Tips: Visit in the morning to sample some of the local bakeries and cafes.

Review: Rue du Faubourg-Poissonnière is a local and authentic shopping street in the heart of Paris's 10th arrondissement, with a mix of local shops, specialty food shops, and bakeries. The street has a lively and authentic atmosphere, especially in the morning when the local bakeries and cafes open their doors.

Getting there: The nearest metro stations are Poissonnière and Gare de l'Est.

RUE DU FAUBOURG-SAINT-ANTOINE

Rue du Faubourg-Saint-Antoine is a historic and artisanal shopping street in Paris, known for its mix of independent shops, craftsmen, and antique dealers.

Address: Rue du Faubourg-Saint-Antoine, 75012 Paris, France

Amenities: Shopping, cafes, restaurants, antique dealers

Stores and Brands: Independent shops selling clothing, accessories, and home goods, as well as craftsmen and antique dealers

Advice: Visit the nearby Place de la Bastille, a historic square with a range of shops, restaurants, and cultural attractions.

Tips: Explore the side streets to discover hidden gems, such as the local craftsmen workshops.

Review: Rue du Faubourg-Saint-Antoine offers a historic and artisanal shopping experience in the heart of Paris's 12th arrondissement, with a mix of independent shops, craftsmen, and antique dealers. The street has a unique and authentic atmosphere, especially in the side streets where you can discover hidden gems.

Getting there: The nearest metro stations are Ledru-Rollin and Faidherbe-Chaligny.

RUE DU FAUBOURG-SAINT-DENIS

Rue du Faubourg-Saint-Denis is a vibrant and multicultural shopping street in Paris, known for its mix of local shops, restaurants, and bars.

Address: Rue du Faubourg-Saint-Denis, 75010 Paris, France

Amenities: Shopping, cafes, restaurants, bars

Stores and Brands: Local shops selling clothing, accessories, and home goods, as well as specialty food shops and bakeries

Advice: Take some time to explore the nearby Canal Saint-Martin, a picturesque waterway lined with cafes and shops.

Tips: Visit in the evening to experience the street's lively atmosphere and bustling bars.

Review: Rue du Faubourg-Saint-Denis offers a vibrant and multicultural shopping experience in the heart of Paris's 10th arrondissement, with a mix of local shops, specialty food shops, and bakeries. The street has a lively and authentic atmosphere, especially in the evening when the bars and restaurants are bustling.

Getting there: The nearest metro stations are Château d'Eau and Strasbourg-Saint-Denis.

RUE DU FAUBOURG-SAINT-MARTIN

Rue du Faubourg-Saint-Martin is a lively and multicultural shopping street in Paris, known for its mix of local shops, restaurants, and cafes.

Address: Rue du Faubourg-Saint-Martin, 75010 Paris, France

Amenities: Shopping, cafes, restaurants, bars

Stores and Brands: Local shops selling clothing, accessories, and home goods, as well as specialty food shops and bakeries

Advice: Explore the nearby Canal Saint-Martin, a picturesque waterway lined with cafes and shops.

Tips: Visit in the evening to experience the street's lively atmosphere and bustling bars.

Review: Rue du Faubourg-Saint-Martin offers a lively and multicultural shopping experience in the heart of Paris's 10th arrondissement, with a mix of local shops, specialty food shops, and bakeries. The street has a lively and authentic atmosphere, especially in the evening when the bars and restaurants are bustling.

Getting there: The nearest metro stations are Château-Landon and Louis Blanc.

RUE DU JOUR

Rue du Jour is a historic and pedestrian shopping street in the heart of Paris, known for its mix of independent shops and cafes.

Address: Rue du Jour, 75001 Paris, France

Amenities: Shopping, cafes, restaurants

Stores and Brands: Independent shops selling clothing, accessories, and home goods

Advice: Visit the nearby Forum des Halles, a modern shopping center with a range of shops and restaurants.

Tips: Explore the side streets to discover hidden gems, such as the local antique shops.

Review: Rue du Jour offers a historic and pedestrian shopping experience in the heart of Paris's 1st arrondissement, with a mix of independent shops and cafes. The street has a unique and authentic atmosphere, especially in the side streets where you can discover hidden gems.

Getting there: The nearest metro station is Les Halles.

RUE DU ROI DE SICILE

Rue du Roi de Sicile is a trendy and stylish shopping street in the heart of Paris, known for its mix of independent boutiques and cafes.

Address: Rue du Roi de Sicile, 75004 Paris, France

Amenities: Shopping, cafes, restaurants

Stores and Brands: Independent boutiques selling clothing, accessories, and home goods

Advice: Visit the nearby Place des Vosges, a historic square with a range of shops, restaurants, and cultural attractions.

Tips: Explore the side streets to discover hidden gems, such as the local galleries and vintage shops.

Review: Rue du Roi de Sicile offers a trendy and stylish shopping experience in the heart of Paris's 4th arrondissement, with a mix of independent boutiques and cafes. The street has a chic and fashionable atmosphere, with a range of unique and stylish shops to discover.

Getting there: The nearest metro station is Saint-Paul.

RUE DU TEMPLE

Rue du Temple is a historic shopping street in the heart of Paris, known for its mix of independent shops and cafes.

Address: Rue du Temple, 75003 Paris, France

Amenities: Shopping, cafes, restaurants

Stores and Brands: Independent shops selling clothing, accessories, and home goods

Advice: Visit the nearby Centre Pompidou, a modern art museum with a range of exhibitions and events.

Tips: Explore the side streets to discover hidden gems, such as the local bookstores and vintage shops.

Review: Rue du Temple offers a historic and authentic shopping experience in the heart of Paris's 3rd arrondissement, with a mix of independent shops and cafes. The street has a unique and charming atmosphere, especially in the side streets where you can discover hidden gems.

Getting there: The nearest metro station is République.

RUE MAZARINE

Rue Mazarine is a historic and upscale shopping street in the heart of Paris, known for its mix of luxury boutiques and art galleries.

Address: Rue Mazarine, 75006 Paris, France

Amenities: Shopping, cafes, restaurants, art galleries

Stores and Brands: Luxury boutiques selling clothing, accessories, and home goods, as well as art galleries and antique shops

Advice: Visit the nearby Jardin du Luxembourg, a picturesque park with a range of gardens, sculptures, and cultural attractions.

Tips: Explore the side streets to discover hidden gems, such as the local chocolate shops and artisanal bookstores.

Review: Rue Mazarine offers an upscale and luxurious shopping experience in the heart of Paris's 6th arrondissement, with a mix of luxury boutiques and art galleries. The street has a sophisticated and elegant atmosphere, with a range of unique and high-end shops to discover.

Getting there: The nearest metro stations are Odéon and Saint-Germain-des-Prés.

RUE OBERKAMPF

Rue Oberkampf is a trendy and lively shopping street in Paris, known for its mix of independent shops, bars, and restaurants.

Address: Rue Oberkpf, 75011 Paris, France

Amenities: Shopping, cafes, bars, restaurants

Stores and Brands: Independent shops selling clothing, accessories, and home goods

Advice: Visit the nearby Place de la Bastille, a historic square with a range of cultural attractions and events.

Tips: Explore the side streets to discover hidden gems, such as the local street art and vintage shops.

Review: Rue Oberkampf offers a trendy and vibrant shopping experience in the heart of Paris's 11th arrondissement, with a mix of independent shops, bars, and restaurants. The street has a lively and youthful atmosphere, with a range of unique and edgy shops to discover.

Getting there: The nearest metro stations are Oberkampf and Parmentier.

RUE SAINT-ANDRÉ DES ARTS

Rue Saint-André des Arts is a historic and lively shopping street in Paris, known for its mix of independent shops, cafes, and cultural attractions.

Address: Rue Saint-André des Arts, 75006 Paris, France

Amenities: Shopping, cafes, restaurants, cultural attractions

Stores and Brands: Independent shops selling clothing, accessories, and home goods, as well as cultural attractions such as theaters and cinemas

Advice: Visit the nearby Musée de Cluny, a medieval art museum housed in a historic building.

Tips: Explore the side streets to discover hidden gems, such as the local art galleries and antique shops.

Review: Rue Saint-André des Arts offers a historic and cultural shopping experience in the heart of Paris's 6th arrondissement, with a mix of independent shops, cafes, and cultural attractions. The street has a charming and lively atmosphere, with a range of unique and interesting shops to discover.

Getting there: The nearest metro stations are Saint-Michel and Odéon.

RUE SAINT-HONORÉ

Rue Saint-Honoré is a historic and luxurious shopping street in Paris, known for its mix of high-end boutiques and luxury hotels.

Address: Rue Saint-Honoré, 75001 Paris, France

Amenities: Shopping, cafes, restaurants, luxury hotels

Stores and Brands: High-end boutiques selling clothing, accessories, and home goods from luxury brands such as Chanel, Dior, and Hermès

Advice: Visit the nearby Louvre Museum, a world-famous art museum housed in a historic building.

Tips: Explore the side streets to discover hidden gems, such as the local art galleries and artisanal shops.

Review: Rue Saint-Honoré offers a luxurious and upscale shopping experience in the heart of Paris's 1st arrondissement, with a mix of high-end boutiques, luxury hotels, and trendy cafes and restaurants. The street has a chic and sophisticated atmosphere, with a range of prestigious brands and designer shops to discover.

Getting there: The nearest metro stations are Concorde, Tuileries, and Pyramides.

RUE SAINT-MAUR

Rue Saint-Maur is a lively and trendy shopping street in Paris, known for its mix of independent shops, cafes, and nightlife.

Address: Rue Saint-Maur, 75011 Paris, France

Amenities: Shopping, cafes, bars, restaurants, nightlife

Stores and Brands: Independent shops selling clothing, accessories, and home goods, as well as vintage and secondhand shops

Advice: Visit the nearby Père Lachaise Cemetery, a historic and beautiful cemetery with a range of notable graves and monuments.

Tips: Explore the side streets to discover hidden gems, such as the local street art and graffiti.

Review: Rue Saint-Maur offers a hip and alternative shopping experience in the heart of Paris's 11th arrondissement, with a mix of independent shops, vintage stores, and trendy bars and restaurants. The street has a lively and creative atmosphere, with a range of unique and edgy shops to discover.

Getting there: The nearest metro stations are Saint-Ambroise and Rue Saint-Maur.

RUE SAINT-PLACIDE

Rue Saint-Placide is a popular shopping street in Paris, known for its mix of high-end and affordable fashion boutiques, as well as its range of beauty shops and gourmet food stores.

Address: Rue Saint-Placide, 75006 Paris, France

Amenities: Shopping, cafes, restaurants, beauty shops, gourmet food stores

Stores and Brands: High-end and affordable fashion boutiques, such as Sandro, Claudie Pierlot, Zara, and COS, as well as beauty shops like L'Occitane and Kiehl's, and gourmet food stores like La Grande Épicerie de Paris

Advice: Take a break from shopping and enjoy a coffee or pastry at one of the many cafes and bakeries along the street.

Tips: Don't miss La Grande Épicerie de Paris, a gourmet food store with a wide range of high-quality products from around the world.

Review: Rue Saint-Placide offers a diverse and upscale shopping experience in Paris's 6th arrondissement, with a mix of high-end and affordable fashion boutiques, beauty shops, and gourmet food stores. The street has a chic and sophisticated atmosphere, with a range of trendy cafes and restaurants to discover.

Getting there: The nearest metro stations are Saint-Placide and Sèvres-Babylone.

Made in the USA
Coppell, TX
28 January 2025

45091069R00049